BRITAIN IN PICTURES
THE BRITISH PEOPLE IN PICTURES

THE BRITISH THEATRE

GENERAL EDITOR
W. J. TURNER

The Editor is most grateful to all those who have
so kindly helped in the selection of illustrations
especially to officials of the various public
Museums Libraries and Galleries and
to all others who have generously
allowed pictures and MSS
to be reproduced

THE
BRITISH THEATRE

BERNARD MILES

WITH
8 PLATES IN COLOUR
AND
21 ILLUSTRATIONS IN
BLACK & WHITE

COLLINS · 14 ST. JAMES'S PLACE · LONDON
MCMXLVIII

1948

PRODUCED BY
ADPRINT LIMITED LONDON

PRINTED IN GREAT BRITAIN BY
CLARKE & SHERWELL LTD NORTHAMPTON
ON MELLOTEX BOOK PAPER MADE BY
TULLIS RUSSELL & CO LTD MARKINCH SCOTLAND

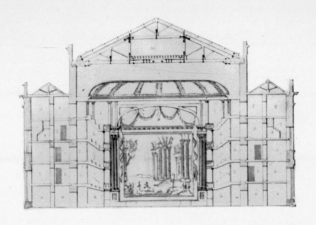

LIST OF ILLUSTRATIONS

PLATES IN COLOUR

A PERFORMANCE AT A COUNTRY BARN THEATRE
Perhaps the Witches' Scene from *Macbeth*
Coloured aquatint by W. R. Pyne after John Wright, 1788

DAVID GARRICK AND MRS. PRITCHARD AS MACBETH
AND LADY MACBETH
Oil painting by Johann Zoffany, *c.* 1768

INTERIOR OF DRURY LANE THEATRE
Detail from a water colour by Edward Dayes, 1795

EDMUND KEAN AS SIR GILES OVERREACH IN
A NEW WAY TO PAY OLD DEBTS
Oil sketch attributed to George Clint, *c.* 1820

SARAH SIDDONS, 1755-1831
Oil sketch by George Romney

SAMUEL PHELPS AS FALSTAFF
Toy Theatre Sheet, *c.* 1860

ELLEN TERRY AS LADY MACBETH
Oil painting by John S. Sargent, 1889

LAURENCE OLIVIER AS ROMEO
Oil painting by Harold Knight, 1936

BLACK AND WHITE ILLUSTRATIONS

PAGE

ELEVATION OF DRURY LANE THEATRE 5
Engraving by J. Le Keux after T. Wyatt
From *Public Buildings of London* by
Britton and Pugin, 1825

TARLTON AS A CLOWN 7
Capital T from an ornamental Elizabethan
alphabet
Probably written by John Scottoue,
c. 1558-1603 [Codex Harley 3885]
By courtesy of the Trustees of the British Museum

RICHARD BURBAGE, 1567-1619 11
Contemporary oil painting by an unknown
artist
*By courtesy of the Governors of Alleyn's College of
God's Gift, Dulwich*

STROLLING PLAYERS IN A SMALL TOWN 13
Engraving by William Faithorne from the
first English edition of Scarron's *Comical
Romance*, 1676

INVITATION TO AN ACTOR'S BENEFIT
PERFORMANCE 15
Etching by William Hogarth, 1697-1764

CHARLES MACKLIN AND MRS. POPE AS
SHYLOCK AND PORTIA IN THE TRIAL SCENE
FROM *THE MERCHANT OF VENICE* 19
Engraving by W. Nutter after J. Boyne,
1790

DAVID GARRICK AS RICHARD III 21
Mezzotint by S. W. Reynolds after a
painting by Nathaniel Dance, 1771

SPRANGER BARRY AS HAMLET AND MRS.
BARRY AS THE QUEEN 23
Oil painting ascribed to James Roberts,
c. 1777
By courtesy of the Garrick Club

JOHN KEMBLE AS HAMLET 25
Pencil drawing by Sir Thomas Lawrence,
c. 1800
*By courtesy of the Trustees of the National Portrait
Gallery*

MRS. ABINGTON AS LADY BETTY MODISH
IN *THE CARELESS HUSBAND* 26
Engraving by L. Taylor, 1777

PAGE

G. F. COOKE AS RICHARD III 27
Engraving after C. R. Leslie, 1756-1812

MASTER BETTY AS YOUNG NORVAL IN
DOUGLAS 28
Oil painting by John Opie, 1805
By courtesy of the Garrick Club

EDMUND KEAN AS CORIOLANUS 31
Engraving after T. C. Wageman, 1820

WILLIAM CHARLES MACREADY AS MAC-
BETH 34
Engraving from Tallis's *Dramatic Maga-
zine*, 1850

SAMUEL PHELPS AS MACBETH 35
Engraving from Tallis's *Dramatic Magazine*, 1850

SIR HENRY IRVING, 1838-1905 37
Oil painting by Jules Bastien-Lepage,
1880
*By courtesy of the Trustees of the National Portrait
Gallery*

TEASING THE GHOST IN *HAMLET* 39
Engraving by George Cruikshank from
G. Raymond's *Life of R. W. Elliston*, 1857

PEGGY ASHCROFT AS ROSALIND IN *AS YOU
LIKE IT* 43
Pencil drawing by W. R. Sickert, 1932
By courtesy of Miss Ashcroft

EDITH EVANS ABOUT TO MAKE HER
ENTRANCE AS QUEEN ELIZABETH IN
HERBERT FARJEON'S *DIVERSION NO. 2* 45
Drawing by Feliks Topolski, 1940
By courtesy of Dame Edith Evans and the Artist

JOHN GIELGUD AS VALENTINE IN *LOVE
FOR LOVE* 47
Oil painting by Anthony Devas, 1943
By courtesy of John Gielgud, Esq., and the Artist

SHAKESPEARE'S GLOBE THEATRE 48
Drawing (based on contemporary information) by Maurice Percival, 1947. With
acknowledgments to J. Cranford Adams's
*The Globe Playhouse, its Design and Equip-
ment.* (Harvard University Press, 1942)

*Illustrations on pp. 15, 21, 26, 27, 31, 34, 35, 39 are reproduced
from engravings in the Author's collection*

The picture here set down
within this letter T:
A right doth shew the forme
of Tharlton vnto the shap
When hee in pleasaunt wise
the Counterfet expreste
of Clowne wt cote of russet-
and shurtups wt crosse, hem.
Whoe merry many mad
when he appeard in sight
The graue and wise as well as
at him did take delight (rude
The partie nowe is gone.
and closlie clad in claye,
Of all the Iesters in the lande
he bare the praise awaie.
Now hath he plaid his pte
and sure he is of this.
If hee in Christe did dieto liue
with him in lasting blis.

TARLTON AS A CLOWN
Capital T from an ornamental Elizabethan alphabet, *c.* 1558-1603

THE BEGINNERS

IN 1483, a Yorkshire actor named Robert Brown was paid sixpence for acting the part of God in the play of *Noah* at Hull. A fine British name, a good strong role, and a fair wage! How better could we begin a book on the British Theatre?

But the first British theatre was already as remote from the theatre of Robert Brown as our own is from that of Shakespeare. For we know that by the end of the twelfth century parts of the church service were being regularly rendered by priests and choristers in the simple question and answer of a primitive drama; and that when the elaborate cycles of mysteries, which grew from these humble roots, had become so popular that

7

the churches were no longer big enough to hold the audiences which flocked to see them, they moved out into the churchyards. One lad, at the end of the thirteenth century, climbed up to the spire of Beverley Minster to get a bird's-eye view of a Resurrection play, but accidentally put his foot on a piece of loose coping and came crashing down amongst the players. His body was carried into the church, where "the Lord desiring to give a living proof to the representation of His own Resurrection, which was meanwhile being played"—and perhaps also desiring to demonstrate His approval of playgoing—"raised the lad up safe and sound in the sight of all."

When the Church began to frown upon this novel form of worship, and at last banned it altogether, the theatre passed into the capable hands of the trade guilds, the greatest social force in mediæval England. The guilds were admirably adapted for their new role, with good organisation, thousands of members and a strong sense of civic responsibility. Each trade undertook a particular play, and levied "pageant pence" upon its members, to defray production costs.

The later mediæval theatre was in fact guild-subsidised, and plays were now performed in market-places and on village greens instead of in churches and churchyards. In order to reach as many people as possible, a simple wagon stage was evolved—"an highe place made like an howse, with two rowmes being open on the top; in the lower rowme they apparelled and dressed themselves; and in the higher rowme they played, and they stood upon wheels." Each play had its own special wagon, open at the front and sides, and backed with a curtain; and these were taken as it were on circuit into various parts of the town and into the surrounding villages. Actors were chosen for their "personne, connynge and voice," and some of the instructions set down for their benefit are as practical as Hamlet's to the Players—"Nor must they foist in a syllable or clip one of the verses, but must enounce firmly and repeat what is set down for them in due order; and whoever names Paradise is to look and point towards it." Actors who did not know their parts were fined.

Effects were elaborate. In a Cornish record we read—"The father must be in a clowde, and when he speaketh of heaven let the levys open." At Chelmsford there is an order for "fyftie fadam of lyne for the cloudes," while Coventry boasted a hell-mouth in the form of a dragon's head belching fire and brimstone. Its jaws were moved with a windlass and into them were driven "bad angyls and black sowles" to the sound of thunder. In one of the Cornish plays, Lucifer "goeth downe to Hell appareled fowle with fyre about him," and the actor who plays Belial is told to "loke that he hath gunne powder brennyng in pypys in his hands and in his ers."

Great care was taken over costumes. In Cornwall, Adam and Eve were "aparlet in white leather, with ffig leaves redy to cover their members." In the Coventry records we read of "a new coat and a peir of hoes for

A PERFORMANCE AT A COUNTRY BARN THEATRE
Perhaps the Witches' Scene from *Macbeth*
Coloured aquatint by W. R. Pyne after John Wright, 1788

DAVID GARRICK AND MRS. PRITCHARD AS MACBETH AND LADY MACBETH

Oil painting by Johann Zoffany, c. 1768

Gabrielle," and at Leicester, "a pound of hemp to mend the angels heads." We also have an order for "a face and heare for the Father"—meaning a mask and wig—the wig to be gilded.

Such was the theatre of Robert Brown, the Yorkshire actor who played God in 1483. At the same performance, Noah and his wife received one and sixpence, the ship-child a penny, the ship-smith ("for clinking Noah's ship") sevenpence, and the waits sixpence ; while straw and grease for the wheels of the wagon cost a farthing. In 1421 a new ship had cost £5 8s. 4d.

Thus, in the days when work, worship and recreation were inseparable, the theatre grew out of the everyday life of the English people, who were its first playwrights, actors, wardrobe mistresses, property masters and stage carpenters. Scenery, costume and make-up were all of local manufacture, and the language of the plays mostly vernacular. In fact, the whole thing was home-grown, owing nothing to the antique models of Greece and Rome. It was rough, simple, sturdy and flexible, and provided an admirable foundation for the mighty structure which followed it.

THE ELIZABETHAN STAGE

WHEN the trade guilds declined, most of the actors took to the roads and tried to support themselves. They became the first strolling players, carrying their scenery and their props on their backs, and performing for whatever they could pick up. Only the luckier and more talented ones found places in those private companies which, as the sixteenth century wore on and play-acting became more popular, were formed by wealthy and cultured noblemen to play in their castles and country houses.

It was to James Burbage, the leading man in one of these companies, that a licence was granted to put up the first real theatre ever built in England. It cost between £600 and £700, was constructed entirely of wood, was opened for public entertainment in the autumn of 1576, and was called simply and appropriately The Theatre.

We don't know very much about The Theatre, but we know a great deal about a later and far more important playhouse, because an American scholar, John Cranford Adams, has recently produced a thrilling book in which he builds up a complete and detailed picture of the shape and size and mode of working of Shakespeare's "Great Globe itself" (built in 1599), and we know that all the Elizabethan playhouses followed much the same pattern.

If you stand in the yard of an old English inn, like the Bull at Rochester, you can easily imagine yourself inside any one of them. The open courtyard is surrounded by three tiers of wide gallery. Thrust out from the end opposite to the entrance is a huge platform extending half-way down the yard and partly covered by a canopy supported on columns, and painted underneath to represent the heavens. At the back, a curtained opening leads to an inner stage used for such scenes as Desdemona's bedchamber or any place "within." Above this is a balcony for scenes taking place "above"—the battlements of Elsinore, or Cleopatra's monument— and over the balcony a music gallery. At each side of the ground-floor opening are doors leading back-stage. In the platform itself are traps for the burying of bodies and the raising of apparitions. The "groundlings" stand solid on three sides of the stage, and pressed right up against it, so that the actor is literally in the midst of his audience instead of at one end of it.

Since the Globe held just over two thousand people, packed into a space not much bigger than Wyndham's Theatre or the Apollo, each of which holds only about nine hundred, to perform in such a theatre must have been comparable to the experience I had in the Orkneys in 1943, playing on a rough platform slung between the destroyers *Orwell* and *Opportune*, with five hundred sailors surrounding the stage and hanging on to every available projection of the two ships. Actors who have had such an experience must realise how much is wasted in the picture-frame theatre of that close union between actor and audience which is the life and soul of the stage.

Performances were announced by play bills "sette upon postes certain dayes before," and more immediately by "the blast of a Trumpette." They began at three o'clock in the afternoon and the theatre flag was flown from the roof while the play was in progress. Prices ranged from 3d. for standing room to a shilling for a seat in a box. The actors wore the costume of their own day, except when performing characters requiring special differentiation. There was no scenery, and only the barest of stage furniture, and all female characters were played by boys.

It is a mistake to suppose the Elizabethan theatre was a sort of glorified fit-up. It was rather the result of three hundred years of trial and error in practical stagecraft. It permitted the play to move swiftly, kept the actors in closest contact with their audience, and allowed the words to work their own magic without heavy-fisted attempts at realistic setting. In fact, it was perfectly adapted to the poetic drama which was produced in it, and which cannot very profitably be studied except in relation to it; and it was a very sad day when it disappeared.

The greatest of the Elizabethan actors was Richard Burbage, son of James Burbage who built The Theatre. Born and brought up in the business, he created many of Shakespeare's greatest characters on the stage of the Globe, and we may take it that Hamlet's advice to the Players gives, in reverse as it were, a faithful impression of his abilities. He was accepted by his own age—an age of powerful imagination, high animal spirits and strong relish of language—as its most truthful imitator. He played roles

RICHARD BURBAGE, 1567-1619
Contemporary oil painting by an unknown artist

which, above everything else, called for actors who could speak thrillingly. And since Elizabethan England was famous throughout Europe for its singing, it is likely that he was vocally superior to any actor before or since. A contemporary speaks of him as "a delightful Proteus, so wholly transforming himself into his part and putting off himself with his clothes, as he never assumed himself again until the play was done"; while an elegy on his death records that

> "every thought and mood
> Might throughly from his face be understood.
> And his whole action he could change with ease,
> From ancient Leare to youthful Pericles."

Almost the equal of Burbage was Edward Alleyn, who founded Dulwich College—"two such actors as no age must ever look to see the like"; while

11

Dick Tarlton, a famous comic, could "force the saddest soul to laughter," and when the Queen herself was sad, could "undumpish her at his pleasure."

But these were only three of the star performers. By the end of the Elizabethan age there were at least a dozen theatres, each with its company of twenty or thirty. Add stage managers, prompters, carpenters, prop men, and front-of-house staff, and it will be seen that the Elizabethan theatre was, in its own small way, an extremely flourishing and popular industry.

We don't know how much the actors earned, because the companies were run on a commonwealth system, all profits being shared after working expenses had been deducted. They gave only two public performances a week, but were doing shows almost every evening at Court or in private houses—in return for food and drink and a whip round. Thus payment was by results, and a stake in the show was part of each actor's birthright. We shall see later on how this birthright was stolen and how the art of the theatre was slowly but surely dragged into the realm of commerce, and how it is only now beginning to escape.

THE RESTORATION

IT must not be supposed that the growth and prosperity of the Eliza-bethan stage went on unopposed. Ever since 1576 Puritan hostility had been intense, for the new religion had no place for joy; and had it not been for royal protection and the support of wealthy patrons, "the fylthie playhouses" would have been closed long before they actually were.

When, in 1642, the order was at last given to shut down, the Puritans committed one of their most unforgivable crimes, because the English theatre had taken three hundred years to grow and because it was a unique structure which could not be replaced once the tradition was broken. The actors fought for the King in the Civil War because they knew that a royal victory was their only hope of bread and butter. When the King lost, those who could find no other way to live had to go hungry and hope for better days. So it is not surprising that when, after eighteen years of Puritan government, the King came back and ushered in the twenty-five years' orgy which we call the Restoration, the theatre was the spearhead of the reaction, and that it more than justified the attacks of its most ferocious critics. It was a period of intense theatrical activity, though of a very limited kind, like a smutty joke intended only for the initiated ; and is chiefly important as a fresh starting-point in the whole theatrical story so violently broken off eighteen years before.

The basic change was in the design of theatres themselves. Looking to France and Italy for their models, instead of to the native playhouses of Bankside, Restoration architects introduced the picture-frame stage, which had often been used at Court, but never in actual theatres. This was a most unhappy innovation; for although the act-drop was kept up throughout the show, and although the actors made all their entrances down-stage and performed almost entirely on the apron, the great platform of the Elizabethan theatre was chopped off short, and there began that long and melancholy retreat of the actor further and further up-stage, until, with the introduction of lamps behind the picture-frame itself, he was finally cut off from the audience altogether, and a playhouse became a combination of two separate rooms, one containing the audience and the other containing the actors, instead of a single structure containing both. And, as if that was not bad enough, the picture-frame stage brought with it painted

STROLLING PLAYERS IN A SMALL TOWN
Engraving by William Faithorne, 1676

scenery, to compete with the spoken word, and to point the way to the senseless attempts of later ages to achieve pictorial illusion.

It has been calculated that the Duke's Theatre in Dorset Gardens, opened in 1671, held about 1,200 people, accommodated in boxes (4s. a seat), pit (2s. 6d.), middle gallery (1s. 6d.), and upper gallery (1s.), and that a full house came to about £120. The play started at half past three, and if you didn't like the first act, you could get your money back and go home. Lighting was by candelabra and scenes were changed in full view of the audience. Armed guards were posted in the vestibule and on the stage itself, to see that no one cheated the box office, and to restore order in the event of a brawl. For the audience were mostly well-to-do and mostly vicious, and as the men usually wore swords and came not to see and hear but to be seen and heard, and to show off their fine clothes and their quick wits and to solicit the women, it is no wonder that there were frequent quarrels or that some of them ended fatally. A contemporary writer describes how he saw a member of the audience receive a mortal wound in the pit of Drury Lane, and how "he presently died, after being removed to a house opposite the theatre." There was at least one attempt to kidnap Mrs. Bracegirdle, the most celebrated actress of the time, while the actor Mountfort was murdered in cold blood because she was thought to have smiled upon him.

The most lively glimpses of the Restoration stage are given by Pepys, who, until he feared he was going blind, was an inveterate playgoer.

1661
January 19th. To the Theatre, where I was troubled to be seen by four of our office clerks, which sat in the half-crowne box and I in the 1s. 6d.

January 28th. To the Theatre, where a lady spit backward upon me by mistake, not seeing me, but after seeing her to be a very pretty lady, I was not troubled at it at all.

1663
February 23rd. To the Duke's house . . . being most pleased to see the little girle dance in boy's apparel, she having very fine legs, only bends in the hams, as I perceive all women do.

1667
November 2nd. To the King's playhouse, and there . . . a gentleman of good habit, sitting just before us, eating of some fruit in the midst of the play did drop down as dead, being choked ; but with much ado Orange Moll did thrust her finger down his throat, and brought him to life again.

The conditions in which the actors of the Restoration had to perform would be unendurable to the modern actor—the guttering candles, the endless chatter and movement of the audience, the fops and the know-alls topping the general hubbub with their running commentary on play and players. And most of the Restoration performances (especially in tragedy) would certainly be unendurable to a modern audience—in a way that the performances of Garrick or Kean or Irving certainly would not. For the new acting, like the new theatres, was copied largely from the French—all sing-song and formal declamation, which is all very well for Corneille and Racine, but not for Shakespeare. Speaking of "the just Delivery of Poetical Numbers," Colley Cibber tells us that "the Voice of a Singer is not more strictly ty'd to Time and Tune, than that of an Actor in Theatrical Elocution."

INVITATION TO AN ACTOR'S BENEFIT PERFORMANCE
Etching by William Hogarth, 1697-1764

The Elizabethan actors had been rehearsed by the poets who wrote the plays. "It was the happiness of the Actors of those Times," we read, "to have such Poets as these to instruct them and write for them ; and no less of those poets, to have such docile and excellent Actors to act their plays." We may be certain that Elizabethan acting was as English as the Elizabethan drama, making use of foreign ideas perhaps, but absorbing them into the native whole, as Shakespeare absorbs Plutarch and Froissart. The Restoration theatre had lost touch with English life and had forgotten its age-old function as popular entertainer. Its dramatists, actors and stage managers simply copied an alien style because the King and the Court demanded it; and this style persisted in the English theatre for eighty years.

Greatest of Restoration actors was Thomas Betterton, the son of a pastry-cook in the royal kitchens, who reigned supreme in the London theatre for half a century. That shrewd theatrical commentator, Colley Cibber, has left us a wonderful account of Betterton's acting. "He seemed," he tells us, "to seize the Eyes and Ears of the Giddy and Inadvertent," so that "to have talked or looked another way would then have been thought Impossibility or Ignorance"—which is the mark of a great stage personality.

15

When, as Hamlet, he first saw his father's ghost, he opened the scene "with a Pause of mute Amazement, then, rising slowly to a solemn trembling Voice he made the Ghost equally terrible to the Spectators as to himself," playing the rest of the scene with "an almost breathless astonishment." But we must remember that the writer of this account accepted stylised speech and gesture as a *sine qua non* of excellence in acting, and I believe Betterton really used his strong personality and his rare physical and imaginative gifts to turn the art of acting into a sort of Bye-path Meadow, from which it was only rescued forty years after his death by the native genius of Garrick.

Far from being a single giant in a histrionic desert, Betterton was surrounded throughout his career by brilliant colleagues, most of whom are admirably hit off by Cibber—"the quick imperious vivacity" of Kynaston (the last of the boy-actresses), "the piercing Tone and uncouth Stateliness" of Sandford, "the soft Civility and empty Eminence" of Mountfort, "the ridiculous Solemnity" of Nokes, "enough to have set a whole Bench of Bishops into a titter," "the elevated Dignity and tempestuous Jealousy" of Mrs. Barry, and "the Youth and Lively Aspect" of Mrs. Bracegirdle— the Ellen Terry of her age and creator of Millamant in Congreve's *Way of the World*—"who threw out such a Glow of Health and Chearfulness, that on the Stage few Spectators that were not past it, could behold her without Desire."

For the comedies of Congreve, Wycherley, Vanbrugh and Farquhar, which require more pure style than any other plays in our language, the new acting was ideal. The actors who grew up to speak such glittering dialogue must have been masters in their own line, and it was certainly no fault of theirs that, towards the turn of the century, the English stage began to go into a decline from which, in some ways, it is only just beginning to recover.

In the first place, the new King who landed at Torbay in 1688 was a Puritan and no theatre-lover, so the stage suddenly ceased to be the plaything of a pleasure-loving Court, and had to turn once more to the general public for support ; having so long neglected its function as popular entertainer, this proved uphill work. On top of this, an all-out attack upon its "Immorality and Profaneness" was suddenly launched by a Nonconformist clergyman named Jeremy Collier, who wrote that as nothing had gone further "in Debauching the Age than the Stage-poets and Play-houses, I thought I could not employ my Time better than by writing against them." He certainly had good grounds for his attack. Plays had been getting steadily dirtier and dirtier. In 1678 (the same year as *The Pilgrim's Progress* was published), Dryden had distinguished himself by producing a play called *The Kind Keeper*, which was so dirty that it had to be withdrawn ; and altogether the line of demarcation between theatre and bawdy-house had become gradually less and less clearly defined.

INTERIOR OF DRURY LANE THEATRE

Detail from a water colour by Edward Dayes, 1795

EDMUND KEAN

AS SIR GILES OVERREACH IN *A NEW WAY TO PAY OLD DEBTS*

Oil sketch attributed to George Clint, *c.* 1820

When Collier's indictment appeared in 1698, its effect was immediate. One or two writers, like Congreve and Vanbrugh, published feeble answers, but the majority, headed by Dryden, agreed that he had taxed them justly, and promised to reform. The trouble was that, when they came to cut out the dirt, they had nothing to put in its place except mock pathos and false heroics ; for the coarseness of Elizabethan and of Restoration drama differ in this—that if you remove it from the one, you still have a world of wonder left, while if you remove it from the other, you have nothing.

It was at this moment of lowered vitality that the theatre was invaded by the first business men, just as the human body is invaded by microbes when its resistance is weakest. The first of these gentlemen who loved the theatre not for what it was, but for what they could make out of it, was a wily and autocratic lawyer named Christopher Rich, and he was to be succeeded by a long line of rogues whom the theatre would have been much better without. A contemporary writer describes the new breed of theatre managers as "money-making persons called Adventurers, who, though entirely ignorant of Theatrical Affairs, are still admitted to a proportionate vote in the Management of them," adding that "while the Theatrical Hive has so many drones in it, the labouring Actors are under the greatest discouragement, if not a direct state of oppression." The sharing system, which for over a hundred years had proved simple, equitable and efficient, was now abolished, and the actors put on fixed salaries. Thus they lost their stake in the show, and the theatre suddenly became a financial battleground of business men versus artists, and, what was far worse, of business men versus business men. For there soon grew up the insidious practice of subletting the theatre lease, which by Garrick's time had already grown into a nuisance, and which is to-day a positive disgrace. For the rent of an average-sized London theatre is at the moment anything between £500 and £750 a week ; and the drama is compelled to feed an army of lessees, sub-lessees, dividend-holders, middlemen, clerks and hangers-on, besides trying to find milk for her legitimate children.

Another disastrous change resulting from this new ownership was in the size of playhouses, which, in order to hold more and more money, became bigger and bigger as the eighteenth century wore on, until Mrs. Siddons could say to a young actress as they stood on the stage of Drury Lane towards the end of the century, "My dear, you are come to act in a wilderness !" The Elizabethan platform had first been curtailed in order to make the uncouth English theatre conform a little more to the genteel models of France and Italy (just as the uncouth genius of Shakespeare was made to conform in a multitude of re-writings and adaptations !). Between 1700 and 1800 it was still further curtailed, until hardly any of the fore-stage remained. Meanwhile "the wilderness" of auditorium was growing bigger and bigger, until the eye and the voice of the actor were fighting a losing battle to express anything at all. That is why all but the most powerful performers began to develop the kind of acting known as "ham"—*i.e.* the externals of acting without its heart.

Another evil result of this change-over from actor-management to adventurer-management was the gradual lengthening of the evening's entertainment until, by 1800, the performance often dragged its weary length through five or six hours, and Covent Garden was carrying a permanent company of 105 actors, singers and dancers, in order to make up the full night's offering of tragedy or comedy, with opera, farce or ballet to follow.

MACKLIN AND GARRICK

THE man who first saw that acting had been getting more and more into a rut since the death of Betterton, was a bad-tempered Irishman named Charles Macklin, who, in 1741, was cast to play Shylock in *The Jew of Venice*—one of the many puerile re-writings of Shakespeare which had held the stage throughout the Restoration. Though it was a long time since it had been performed, it was well known that Shylock had always been played as a buffoon, and it was presumed that Macklin would follow suit. But in the face of intense opposition and a good deal of ridicule, he not only restored much of the original Shakespearian text, but insisted on playing Shylock as a real character.

"In the scene where, for the first time, he misses his daughter, he appears without his hat, with his hair standing on end, in some places at least a finger's length above the crown, as if the wind from the gallows had blown it up. Both hands are firmly clenched, and all his movements are abrupt and convulsive. To see such emotion in a grasping, fraudulent character, generally cool and self-possessed, is fearful."

His performance was a tremendous success, and established its creator as one of the outstanding actors of his century.

Macklin was independent, obstinate, and overbearing. In 1735 he narrowly escaped hanging for killing a fellow actor in the Green Room of Drury Lane, in a dispute over a wig ; and such was his facility in making enemies that, in 1773, while playing at Covent Garden, there was a conspiracy to drive him from the London stage altogether. It was considered that the character of Macbeth was the perquisite of an actor named Smith. But Macklin had made it clear from the start that it was one of the parts he intended to play during his engagement. So a small band of mischief-makers organised a hostile demonstration, and when Macklin appeared on the stage, he was greeted with hisses, cat-calls and rotten apples. Then the audience started roaring for him to be sacked, and at last the manager, fearing for his own skin, came in front of the curtain and announced that, as his object was "always to please the public and to conform to their pleasure, when he knew what their pleasure was," their wishes had been obeyed, and the offending actor dismissed!

But Macklin was not so easily defeated, and rather than submit he went to law, proceeding against the ringleaders of the conspiracy with such vigour that, in 1775, Lord Mansfield delivered his famous verdict in the plaintiff's favour.

"Every man that is at the playhouse has a right to express his approbation or disapprobation instantaneously according as he likes either the acting or the piece; that is a right due to the theatre—an unalterable right; they must have that. The gist of the crime here, is

MACKLIN AND MRS. POPE AS SHYLOCK AND PORTIA
Engraving by W. Nutter after J. Boyne, 1790

coming by conspiracy to ruin a particular man—to hiss, if they were ever so pleased—let him do ever so well they were to knock him down and hiss him off the stage."

Although he could easily have got heavy damages, Macklin was content to settle for £300, to be spent by the defendants on tickets for the theatre where he was engaged! This incident shows to what depths the managers had already sunk in pandering to their audiences.

It is said that Macklin had three pauses, "the moderate, the long and the grand," and that he once rushed off-stage and knocked the prompter down for having interrupted him in the middle of his "grand pause"! And that the audience burst into applause when he reappeared! He played Shylock when he was ninety and was nearly a hundred when he died. As he grew older, he grew more and more cantankerous, and spent most of his time slinging mud at the man who is still accepted as our greatest actor—David Garrick.

Garrick was born in Hereford in 1716, but passed his boyhood in Lichfield, where he was taught Latin and Greek by Samuel Johnson, who

19

was running an academy for young gentlemen in a near-by village. In 1737, when the academy closed down, master and pupil set off to try their luck in London. After one or two false starts, Garrick appeared as Richard III at a little theatre in Goodman's Fields, Stepney, at six o'clock on the evening of October 19th, 1741—billed simply as "A Gentleman who never appeared on any stage."

His success was immediate—his whole conception was so fresh and daring, yet so completely convincing. It was said that his voice was "neither whining, bellowing, nor grumbling, but perfectly easy in its transitions, natural in its cadence, and beautiful in its elocution. He is not less happy in his mien and gait, in which he is neither strutting nor mincing, neither stiff nor slouching. When three or four are on the stage with him, he is attentive to whatever is spoke, and never drops his character when he has finished a speech, by either looking contemptuously on an inferior performer, unnecessary spitting, or suffering his eyes to wander through the whole circle of spectators."

Garrick dominated the London stage from the time he went into management at Drury Lane in 1747, until his retirement thirty years later. He brought the same exceptional powers of characterisation to nearly every part he played. He was great in comedy as well as tragedy, as Benedick and Abel Drugger as well as in Lear and Hamlet. He understood that acting is make-believe and that the surest way to make people believe a thing is to tell them the truth about it; that the greatest actors are those whose insight and imagination enables them to tell the most truth about the characters they are representing, or else to bring up to date the truth that has already been told. For the reality of which acting is the mirror is constantly changing, and what was true acting yesterday is not necessarily true to-day.

A contemporary writer who saw Garrick's production of *Macbeth* says that he and Mrs. Pritchard played the scene after Duncan's murder "in terrifying whispers. Their looks and action supplied the place of words. You heard what they spoke, but you learned more from the agitation of mind displayed in their action and deportment."

I believe that Garrick's greatest claim to genius was precisely this filling-in of "looks, action and deportment" between the lines. Following Macklin's example, he set English acting free from declamation (the legacy of the French-inspired Restoration) and made his most powerful effects quite apart from the words. He first grasped that the core of acting lies in the pause, during which the actor loosens or tightens the cords of suspense and raises that expectation which is the life and soul of the theatre.

Garrick was small, but graceful and well-proportioned, with fine dark eyes (great actors have all had wonderful eyes). It is said that Nature had done so much for him "that he could not help being an actor—she gave him a frame of so manageable a proportion, and so perfectly under

DAVID GARRICK AS RICHARD III
Mezzotint by S. W. Reynolds after a painting by Nathaniel Dance, 1771

command, that he could suit it to any sort of character—his eye was so penetrating, so speaking, his brow so moveable, and all his features so plastic and accommodating, that wherever his mind impelled them they

21

would go, and before his tongue could give the text his countenance would express the spirit and passion of the part he was charged with."

Although he restored much of the original text of *Macbeth* (Quin asked him where he had stolen all the wonderful new lines, especially the lovely one about the "cream-fac'd loon" !), he turned *A Midsummer Night's Dream* into a ballad-opera, and his acting version of *Hamlet* was so corrupt that he never dared to print it ; but in this he was typical of his own and later ages, which all considered Shakespeare unfit for human consumption until pre-digested. Indeed a foreigner might well find this the most striking thing about the British theatre—that for two hundred and fifty years after the Restoration scarcely a single play by the world's greatest dramatist reached the stage in its original form !

Besides making a great advance in the art of acting, Garrick made many reforms in the conduct of the theatre itself. He insisted on actors being early for rehearsals and taking them seriously, and cleared the stage of spectators, who by the 1740's were often planted so thick about the wings that players were hard put to it to elbow their way on to the scene. A bishop once asked him why the churches were so empty and the theatres so full. "Because," replied Garrick, "you speak a truth as if it were a fiction, while we speak a fiction as if it were a truth." It was this firm grasp of truth that kept him far ahead of all his competitors, and which drew from Johnson the exquisite epitaph that his death had "eclipsed the gaiety of nations, and impoverished the common stock of harmless pleasures."

The Garrick period is full of brilliant performers, both supporting the master and disputing with him for supremacy. Chief of these was James Quin, leader of the old heroic school, who had said at Garrick's first appearance, "If this young fellow is right, then we have all been wrong !" and who put up a stiff fight before he yielded and retired. He killed two fellow actors in his lifetime—both in self-defence. The first was maddened because Quin refused to praise one of his performances, and insisted on settling the matter with swords ! The second, a Welshman, lost his temper when told that his pronunciation of the word "Cato"—which he rendered as "Keeto"—was offensive to the ear, waylaid Quin after the play, and fell in the ensuing scuffle. Garrick's second rival, Spranger Barry, was a young Irishman with a glorious voice and an "amorous harmony of feature" which Garrick could not supply. His "soft melody and noble ardour" were irresistible in heroes and lovers, but he came to grief when he tried Lear, and eventually gave up the contest. Lastly, there was Samuel Foote, "the English Aristophanes," a great wit, a great mimic, and a great rogue, hated and feared for his wicked imitations of living celebrities, but remembered for a hundred delightful sallies. When the drunken Duke of Norfolk asked him in what new character he should go to a masquerade, Foote replied, "Why not go sober ?", and when the Duke of Cumberland said to him one evening before the show, "Well, Foote, here I am, ready as usual to swallow

SPRANGER BARRY AS HAMLET AND MRS. BARRY AS THE QUEEN
Oil painting ascribed to James Roberts, *c.* 1777

all your good things," Foote answered, "Your Royal Highness must have an excellent digestion, for you never bring any up again."

Garrick's most brilliant leading lady was Mrs. Cibber, for whom Handel wrote the contralto arias in the *Messiah*, and who sang them at its first London performance at Covent Garden in 1743. She married Colley Cibber's beast of a son, Theophilus, who sold her to a gentleman of fortune for four hundred pounds, and when she objected to this arrangement and ran away with a lover, fetched her home by force, claiming five thousand pounds compensation for injury to his honour! In tragedy she rivalled Garrick himself, and her Ophelia was said to be the finest ever seen. Peggy Woffington, the early love who very nearly became his wife; Frances Abington, in Garrick's own words "as silly as she was false and treacherous," but, like our own incomparable Edith Evans, able to "seize upon the exact cadence and emphasis by which the point of the dialogue is enforced"; and Kitty Clive, "a mixture of combustibles and a diamond of the first water," were all great in various lines of comedy, and vied with each other in making Garrick's life a perpetual torment, in a way that only leading actresses know how!

THE KEMBLES AND ONE OR TWO OTHERS

GARRICK founded no school and had no immediate successor. John Henderson, the one actor who might have filled the throne, was cut off at the age of twenty-eight by an accidental overdose of sleeping-draught administered by his wife, and it was left to Sarah Siddons to restore acting to its old glory.

She was the daughter of Roger Kemble, the strolling actor-manager whose children and grandchildren—Sarah, John, Stephen, Charles, Fanny and Adelaide—between them made the family name one of the most famous in theatrical history. Born at Brecon in 1755, she went on the stage as soon as she could walk. By 1772 she was playing leads, and in 1773 married a member of her father's Company, named William Siddons. In 1775, word of her great beauty and exceptional gifts reached Garrick, who invited her to Drury Lane. She made her London début on December 29th, 1775, as Portia, but was too overcome by nerves to do herself justice. Later she played Anne Neville to Garrick's Richard, and incurred the little man's displeasure for up-staging him; but once again was too terrified to make any strong impression, and was driven back to do another seven years' drudgery in the provinces before finally breaking into the London theatre for good. Years afterwards she spoke of "all that labour of mind and body which I wonder I had the strength and courage to bear."

But when at last she reappeared in 1782, she knocked London flat, and thereafter her career was one long triumph. She was gifted with great intelligence, a tall and splendid figure, fine features, wonderful eyes and a magnificent voice, full of tenderness and mystery as well as power. Hazlitt says that she was like "a being of a superior order, dropped from another sphere to awe the world with the majesty of her appearance. Power was seated on her brow; passion emanated from her breast as from a shrine." That she was capable of a terrifying intensity is clear from a story told by Macready. He describes how, in Rowe's *Tamerlane*, when her lover is strangled before her face, "she worked herself up to such a pitch of agony, and gave such terrible reality to the few convulsive words she tried to utter as she sank a lifeless heap before the murderer, that the audience for a few moments remained in a hush of astonishment, as if awe-struck; they then clamoured for the curtain to be dropped, and insisting on the Manager's appearance, received from him, in answer to their vehement en-quiries, the assurance that Mrs. Siddons was alive, and recovering from the temporary indisposition that her exertions had caused. They were satisfied as regarded her, but would not suffer the performance to be resumed."

Sarah's private life was boring and conventional. Meeting her at a party in 1787, Fanny Burney describes her as "sublime, elevated and solemn; in face and person truly noble and commanding; in manner quiet and stiff; in voice deep and dragging; and in conversation formal, sententious, calm and dry. I expected her to have been all that is interesting. But I was very much mistaken." How different from her description of Garrick calling round one morning to talk to her father while he was having his wig dressed; pulling faces at the hairdresser, pretending to auction Dr. Burney's valuable books for a penny apiece, taking off Boswell, and finally giving a superb imitation of Dr. Johnson, "arranging his dress so as to enlarge his person several inches beyond its natural

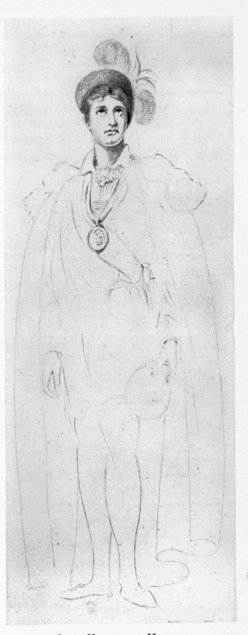

JOHN KEMBLE AS HAMLET
Pencil drawing by Sir Thomas Lawrence, c. 1800

size, assuming the voice and authoritative power of the lexicographer, and giving a thundering stamp on the carpet" by way of prelude.

Although courted by kings and queens, and sought out by the highest in the land, Sarah Siddons was detested by her colleagues for her meanness and her arrogance. She refused to play for her own son's benefit without a guarantee of half the receipts, and was once observed standing next to the Duke of Wellington, silent and haughty—waiting for him to speak first!

Her acting displayed the classical at its best—life and passion controlled by order and dignity. Her brother, John Kemble, represented order and dignity as ends in themselves, and is one of the best examples of everything that the Romantic spirit revolted against. Cold, dignified, cultured and correct, he looked "like a man just about to sneeze." Magnificent in such

MRS. ABINGTON AS LADY BETTY MODISH IN
THE CARELESS HUSBAND
Engraving by L. Taylor, 1777

roles as Cato and Coriolanus, in which an impression of intellectual superiority is half the battle, he was devoid of humanity, and Hazlitt says that he played Hamlet "like a man in armour, with a determined inveteracy of purpose, in one undeviating straight line." We can understand something of his character when we learn that he once repeated 1,500 lines of Homer by heart without a single mistake, that he is known to have written out the entire part of Hamlet forty times and that when he resigned from the stage-management of Drury Lane he made the following speech: "I am an eagle, whose wings have been bound down by frosts and snows; but I now shake my pinions and cleave into the genial air unto which I was born."

26

Although they held such a powerful sway over the London stage for
so many years, the Kembles did not
have matters all their own way. Two
of their most brilliant contempora-
ries, Dora Jordan and George
Frederick Cooke, managed to steal
a good share of the limelight, while
a third, the infant prodigy Master
Betty, contrived for a brief season
to outshine them all.

Dora Jordan was an Irish girl
with a genius for comedy and a
streak of nature which Mrs. Siddons
could not compete with. Hazlitt tells
us that "her face, her tones, her
manner were irresistible; her smile
had the effect of sunshine, and her
laugh did one good to hear; her
voice was eloquence itself — it
seemed as if her heart were always
at her mouth. She was all gaiety,
openness and good nature; she
rioted in her fine animal spirits, and
gave more pleasure than any other
actress because she had the greatest
spirit of enjoyment in herself."
Thomas Campbell tells us that

G. F. COOKE AS RICHARD III
Engraving after C. R. Leslie, 1756-1812

Shakespeare himself would have saluted her Rosalind, and Lamb's description of her Viola is an object-lesson which should be written in letters a
foot high over every actress's bed.

"There is no giving an account," he writes, "how she delivered the
disguised story of her love for Orsino. It was no set speech that she had
foreseen, so as to weave it into a harmonious period, line necessarily following line, to make up the music. . . . When she had declared her sister's
history to be 'a blank,' and 'that she never told her love,' there was a pause,
as if the story had ended ; and then the image of the 'worm i' the bud'
came up as a new suggestion, and the brightened image of 'patience' still
followed after that, as by some growing, and not mechanical process,
thought springing up after thought, I would almost say, as they were
watered by her tears."

The story of her liaison with the Duke of Clarence is well known. She
lived with him for many years, lent him large sums of money and bore him
a whole tribe of children, only to be deserted without a word of explanation,

27

and left to die in misery, awaiting hourly a letter of reconciliation which never arrived.

George Frederick Cooke was born about 1755, went on the stage when he was twenty and, after a long and hard apprenticeship in the provinces, appeared at Covent Garden in 1800 as Richard III. He was immediately hailed as the greatest Gloucester since Garrick, and when he followed up with a Shylock, an Iago and a Sir Giles Overreach every bit as good, the impression was confirmed.

A man of powerful physique and huge voice, he was limited in range to the sardonic and the malignant. But, like Macklin, he showed the way back from the "laboured artifice" into which acting had once again sunk, towards a fresh truth and reality; and there are many accounts of "the terrible visage and short, abrupt and savage utterance" which gave such extraordinary conviction to his acting.

There is a wonderful story told of Cooke. Playing at Liverpool on one occasion (in those days one of the most

MASTER BETTY AS YOUNG NORVAL IN *DOUGLAS*
Oil painting by John Opie, 1805

28

active centres of the slave trade) he was so late getting into the theatre that the audience refused to let the play start until he had made a public apology for holding the curtain. When at last he was able to make himself heard through the uproar, he walked down-stage and spoke the following words to the assembled gentry of Liverpool: "You contemptible money-getters! You shall never again have the honour of hissing *me*! I banish *you*! There is not a single stone of your blasted city that is not cemented with the blood of a slave!" He then walked off the stage and left the theatre!

Cooke drank recklessly, and in the end died of drink. But he could be a most delightful companion and is one of the most lovable of English actors, as well as one of the most gifted.

William Henry West Betty was born in 1791. In 1802 he saw Mrs. Siddons perform in Belfast, and immediately conceived a passion to become an actor. His parents encouraged his ambition, and after a few lessons in elocution and deportment he made his professional début. Such was his success that he was very soon offered an engagement at Covent Garden at £50 a night. At his first performance the theatre was chock-a-block a few minutes after the doors had been opened, and so great was the press in Bow Street that the military had to be called out.

London went crazy over him, and while the mania lasted the Kembles and Cooke and Dora Jordan played to empty benches. When he fell ill, bulletins were issued announcing his latest condition, and William Pitt even moved the motion of adjournment in the House of Commons one evening so that members could go and see him act! But his success was shortlived. When he returned to London for a second season, the craze was over. At fifteen he retired on his winnings, and although a few years afterwards he reappeared, he could make no headway, and eventually gave up for good. Fox said that his Hamlet was finer than Garrick's, and others pronounced verdicts equally extravagant, but serious critics were not taken in. Thomas Campbell says that "the popularity of that baby-faced boy who possessed not even the elements of a good actor, was an hallucination in the public mind and a disgrace to our theatrical profession."

KEAN AND MACREADY

JOHN KEMBLE and Sarah Siddons continued to reign as England's leading players until January 26th, 1814, when all London was electrified by a twenty-seven-year-old strolling tragedian named Edmund Kean—whose playing of Shakespeare Coleridge described as "reading it by flashes of lightning."

Of uncertain parentage, born and bred in the gutter, subjected until the very hour of his London triumph to every kind of misery, privation and disappointment, he had all the actor's gifts except pure inches—the penetrating eye, the stirring and heartbreaking voice, tigerish grace of movement, and a mixture of fiery and melancholy temperament—all forged into a perfect instrument by years of unremitting work. He could dance and sing and tumble, and was one of the best swordsmen of his day ; and, in order to satisfy a public taught to expect the sensational as its birthright, he drove his acting into realms of frenzied passion hitherto unexplored by the actor, and raised his everyday life to the same intense pitch.

His opening performance as Shylock was followed by a Richard III, a Hamlet, an Othello, an Iago, a Macbeth and a Romeo, all full of the rarest beauties and most startling contrasts, which established him as the greatest actor since Garrick.

Of all the descriptions of his acting, Leigh Hunt's analysis of his dying scenes is perhaps the finest, and shows how strenuously and with what detail he imagined each creation. As Richard, he was "reduced to a state resembling the stupor of intoxication—he falls from exhaustion—and as loss of blood may be presumed to cool his frame and restore his sanity, so does he grow calmer and calmer through the dying speech, till his mighty heart is hushed for ever.

"In Othello, death is occasioned by piercing himself to the heart with a poignard ; can you not mark the frozen shudder as the steel enters his frame, and the choking expression with distended eyes and open mouth, the natural attendants of such an agony ? Death by a heart wound is instantaneous. Thus does he portray it ; he literally dies standing ; it is the dead body only of Othello that falls, heavily and at once ; there is no rebound which speaks of vitality and of living muscles. It is the dull weight of clay seeking its kindred earth.

"But the scene that actors admire most, is his death in Hamlet. The Prince does not die of a sword-wound, but from the poison impregnated in that wound ; of course, from its rapidity in doing the work of death, it must have been a powerful mineral. What are the effects of such a poison ? Intense internal pain, wandering vision, swelling veins in the temple. All this Kean details with awful reality. His eye dilates and then loses lustre ; he gnaws his hand in the vain effort to repress emotion ; the veins thicken in his forehead ; his limbs shudder and quiver, and as life grows fainter and his hand drops from between his stiffening lips, he utters a cry of expiring nature, so exquisite that I can only compare it to the wail of a suffering child."

"Who that ever heard," writes Fanny Kemble, "will ever forget the beauty, the unutterable tenderness of his reply to Desdemona's entreaties for Cassio—'Let him come when he will ; I can deny thee nothing !', the deep despondency of his 'Oh, now forever farewell,' the miserable anguish of his 'Oh, Desdemona, away, away !' Who that ever saw will ever forget the fascination of his dying eyes in Richard when deprived of his sword ;

the wondrous power of his look seemed yet to avert the uplifted arm of Richmond."

I think that Kean owed a great part of his strength as an actor to the fact that, although quite at ease in the noblest company, throughout his life he kept in close contact with the gutter and with those raw and coarse fruits of human nature which grow there so abundantly. No great actor before or after him ever had such a near acquaintance with the seamy side of life, or used it to such effect in the delineation of good and evil. It is said that he sacrificed unity of conception to his passion for violent contrast — Hazlitt says "he was too often in the highest key, too uniformly on the verge of extravagance, too constantly on the rack." Also he failed as a comedian. But at his best he was unsurpassed and unsurpassable.

EDMUND KEAN AS CORIOLANUS
Engraving after T. C. Wageman, 1820

He had a wonderful faculty for looking at every characterisation afresh. Hazlitt describes how, as Hamlet, it was he who first thought of pointing his sword backwards when telling the Ghost to lead on—to keep his friends from restraining him, not to protect himself from his father's spirit; and how, at the end of the "nunnery" scene, he suddenly rushed back "after he had gone to the extremity of the stage, from a pang of parting tenderness, to press his lips to Ophelia's hand. It was the finest commentary that was ever made on Shakespeare. It explained the character at once as one of disappointed hope, of bitter regret, of affection suspended, not obliterated, by the destruction of the scene around him."

The last scenes of his life are indescribably moving. The demands made by such reckless expenditure of mind and body could only be met by deeper and deeper draughts of brandy, and at forty he was already a tottering old man. When Helen Faucit was a little girl, she met him on Richmond Green, a white-haired figure with flashing dark eyes, being taken for a walk by his faithful friend Miss Tidswell. Yet he was only just over forty years old. He eventually collapsed in the arms of his son, Charles, while playing Othello at Drury Lane in March 1833, and his death, seven weeks afterwards, left a gap which remained unfilled until the appearance of Henry Irving in 1871.

William Charles Macready, sober, priggish and dictatorial, who never wanted to go on the stage, and who never disguised his contempt for it, was generally accepted as Kean's successor, and was undoubtedly an actor of great power. But acting was contrary to his true nature, and he never captured the popular imagination. He referred to Kean as "that low fellow," and considered that "to be a great actor it was advisable to become a good scholar, an accomplished gentleman, and a well-ordered man, with a well-regulated mind and finely-cultivated taste." But many of his creations, particularly in the blank-verse effusions of Byron and Sheridan Knowles, were tremendously powerful, and even Kean knew better than to try a fall with him, except when he played Othello to Macready's Iago—and with that wonderful last act even a moderate Othello must annihilate the best of Iagos !

All his life Macready longed to be accepted as an intellectual, and when he retired, putting away his make-up box without a tear, he went to live in Cheltenham, where he could enjoy the kind of society he had so long hungered for !

A more versatile actor and a far more lovable man was Samuel Phelps, whose memorable and heroic tenure of the old Sadler's Wells Theatre from 1844 to 1862 provides one of the most stirring episodes in all theatrical history.

PHELPS, IRVING AND ELLEN TERRY

PHELPS was born in 1804 and went on the stage in 1823. After an arduous provincial apprenticeship he won his way to London, where for six years he worked with Macready at Covent Garden, Drury Lane and the Haymarket. In 1844 he joined forces with a couple of colleagues and started in management on his own account at an old playhouse in North London which had "sunk to the lowest ebb" and was given over to "as ruffianly an audience as London could shake together," but which will for ever be coupled with his name—Sadler's Wells.

The opening play was *Macbeth*, and Charles Dickens, who was present, tells us that it was performed "amidst the usual hideous medley of fights, foul language, cat-calls, shrieks, howls, oaths, blasphemy, obscenity, apples, oranges, nuts, biscuits, ginger-beer, porter and pipes. Cans of beer with

SARAH SIDDONS, 1755 - 1831
Oil sketch by George Romney

MR PHELPS as SIR JOHN FALSTAFF N° 74.
London Published by J. REDINGTON, 73 Hoxton Street. Formerly called 208 Hoxton Old Town.

SAMUEL PHELPS AS FALSTAFF
Toy Theatre Sheet, *c.* 1860

a pint measure to drink from, were carried through the dense crowd at all stages of the tragedy. Sickly children in arms were squeezed out of shape in all parts of the house. Fish was fried at the entrance doors, barricades of oyster shells encumbered the pavement. Expectant half-price visitors to the gallery howled defiant impatience up the stairs and danced a sort of carmagnole all round the building."

Undeterred, Phelps set about cleaning the place up. "The fryers of fish, vendors of oysters, and other costermonger scum accumulated round the floors, were first got rid of ; then the noisy sellers of beer inside the theatre, and finally the children in arms." In order to stem the tide of filthy language which nightly rolled across the footlights, Phelps "routed out an old Act of Parliament in which there was a clause visiting the use of bad language in any public place with a fine when the offence was proved before a magistrate. This clause he had printed on great placards and posted up in various conspicuous parts of the theatre. He also had it printed on small hand-bills. To every person who went into the gallery, one of these hand-bills was given with his pass ticket, and he was seriously warned that the Act would be enforced, and it was enforced with such rigour, that on several occasions Mr. Phelps stopped the play to have an offender removed ; on other occasions he went into the gallery with a cloak over his theatrical dress, to point out some other offender who had escaped the vigilance of the police. On all occasions he kept his purpose and his inflexible determination steadily to carry it out ; on no occasion did he show fear or favour." Faced with such resolute opposition, the audience wilted and at last gave in.

In his first season he presented *Hamlet*, *King John*, *The Merchant of Venice*, *Othello* and *Richard III*, besides plays by Beaumont and Fletcher, Massinger and Sheridan. Within seven years he had acted Shakespeare over a thousand nights, and Macready was driven to write, "I believe we must look for the Drama, if we really want to find it, in that remote suburb of Islington."

He collected a strong team of players, and did his best to stick to them. He rehearsed only four hours each day—from ten o'clock until two—and arranged the repertoire so as to spread the donkey-work as evenly as possible. Dickens tells us that "the smallest character in every play has been respectfully approached and studied ; the smallest accessory has been well considered ; every artist in his degree has been taught to adapt his part, in the complete effect to all the other parts, uniting to make up the whole." In this spirit he continued for eighteen years and, in his own words, "succeeded in making a wretched tumble-down suburban theatre the intellectual centre of this mighty metropolis, and therefore, to some extent, the centre of the world." During this time he produced no less than thirty-two of Shakespeare's plays, including such rarities as *Cymbeline*, *Timon of Athens*, *Pericles* and *All's Well that Ends Well*.

33

MACREADY AS MACBETH
Engraving from Tallis's *Dramatic Magazine*, 1850

Phelps was certainly not a great actor in the sense that Garrick and Kean were. He was really the first of modern actors, subjecting himself to the character rather than using the character to exhibit himself; just as he was one of the first people to try and build up something solid and lasting in the way of a company and a method of work. And it is for the miracle he wrought at Sadler's Wells that he is chiefly remembered.

About 1855, a young amateur named Brodribb, who later changed his name to Irving, gave Phelps an audition, and was offered an engagement at Sadler's Wells on the strength of it. But he chose to start his professional career in the provinces, making his first appearance as Gaston, Duke of Orleans, in Bulwer's *Richelieu*, on September 29th, 1856, at the Lyceum, Sunderland.

After playing nearly six hundred roles in the provinces, he eventually got to London, and his performance of Mathias in *The Bells* on November 25th, 1871, immediately stamped him as the most important actor since Kean, and from the time he went into management himself in 1878, until his death in 1905, he was acknowledged as the leader of the London stage.

Irving had the will and imagination of a great actor, without the physical apparatus that should have gone with it. In particular, his vocal deficiencies largely incapacitated him from playing the great tragic heroes of Shakespeare—Coriolanus, Othello, Macbeth, Antony and Hotspur—by which the stature of the greatest actors must in the end be judged. But his personality was so strong, and his dramatic sense so acute, that he was able to substitute values of personal magnetism and stagecraft for the gifts which he lacked, and the result was a series of the most thrilling performances since the death of Kean.

As a great stage-craftsman, his real love was melodrama, and although his Hamlet, Richard III and Shylock were three supreme performances, he only adventured thirteen times into Shakespeare during his whole thirty-one years at the Lyceum. His fault as a manager (which was his great strength as an actor) was that he lived completely in the past, and quite failed to realise that the labours of Phelps and Macready had blown to pieces the whole idea of star acting as it had existed in the palmy days of Kean and the Kembles. When William Terriss stopped the dress rehearsal of *Louis XI*, banged his chest and shouted up to the electrician on the switchboard, "Here, Tom, old man, here I am! Not all on the Guv'nor, you know!" he was making an historical comment as well as a plea for impartiality!

During his long tenure of the Lyceum Irving was partnered by Ellen Terry, one of the most entrancing women ever born—a unique commingling of emotion and intelligence with a glorious face and lovely figure. Like Mrs. Bracegirdle, only much more beautiful, she had such an abundance of health and radiant life, and was such a fountain of pure charm, that it was impossible to behold her without desiring her. But her success depended not only upon her personality and physical beauty, but, like Irving's, upon a hard training and the exercise of a brilliant critical faculty which shows itself most clearly in her autobiography— one of the most fascinating of all theatre books, and the one work which, above all others, convinces me of the genius of Henry Irving. Writing of his Romeo she says, "It is not usual, I think, to make much of the Rosaline episode. Henry Irving chose with great care a tall dark girl to represent Rosaline at the ball. Can I ever forget

SAMUEL PHELPS AS MACBETH
Engraving from Tallis's *Dramatic Magazine*, 1850

35

his face when suddenly in pursuit of *her* he saw *me*. . . . Once more I reflect that a *face* is the chiefest equipment of the actor." Of his death as Mathias she writes, "He did really almost die—he imagined death with such horrible intensity. His eyes would disappear upwards, his face grow grey, his limbs cold." Lastly, the sentence in which she describes his performance in *Madame Sans Gêne*—one of the most searching things ever written about acting—"It seems to me some nights as if I were watching Napoleon trying to imitate Henry Irving."

EXPANSION AND DEVELOPMENT

ALL through the eighteenth century there were still only two chief theatres in London—Drury Lane and Covent Garden, the two Patent Houses, each holding a licence (or patent) granted by Charles II. Smaller houses like Goodman's Fields and the Little Haymarket Theatre sprang up in the early years of the century, and might have become serious competitors to the two major theatres, but for a series of political satires produced at the Haymarket in the early 1730's. These led to the Theatres Act of 1737 which imposed regular censorship on all playwrights, and restricted the legitimate drama to the two major playhouses. Other theatres could only perform opera, pantomime or burlesque. This restriction of straight plays to Drury Lane and Covent Garden continued until 1843 when, after long and vigorous agitation, both the Haymarket and the Lyceum were granted a licence.

With the turn of the century, London began to grow from a reasonable-sized city into the "Great Wen," and there naturally started a wave of theatre-building designed to meet the enormous increase in population. This went on unchecked right up till 1930. From Astley's Amphitheatre (1792), the Olympic and the Adelphi (1806), the Surrey (1809), the Lyceum (1816), the Royal Coburg (1818), they continued in a steady stream, well over a hundred strong, until we reach the Phoenix, Prince Edward—now the Casino—Whitehall and Cambridge (all 1930), and the Saville (1931). Their general pattern remains constant, except that in the latest examples the proscenium boxes are abandoned in favour of an expanse of blank wall. The practice of springing boxes and circles out of the very picture-frame itself so as to preserve living contact between actors and audience was at any rate a sensible hangover from the all-round contact of the Elizabethan stage. But recent architects have presented the actor with the problem of bridging a 20–30-foot gap before his voice and face and personality can begin to register. The Shakespeare Memorial Theatre at Stratford on Avon is an excellent example of a modern building put up without reference to the actor's means of expression, and succeeds in violating all the known principles of communication between performer and audience.

SIR HENRY IRVING, 1838-1905
Oil painting by Jules Bastien-Lepage, 1880

The first big development in the nineteenth-century theatre was in the realm of lighting. The introduction of gas from 1803 onwards meant that house-lights could be lowered, and stage lighting dimmed and increased at will, for the first time in the history of the theatre. The actor's cry for more and more light is not the voice of conceit, but the voice of self-preservation. If he cannot hold the eye of the audience, he is lost. Gaslight meant that the actor could be more easily seen, and that he need not exaggerate his visual effects so strongly as hitherto. Electric light (1881 onwards), and particularly the individual spotlight, was the answer to every actor's prayer, making it possible to select and to isolate the important moment in an entirely new way, and gradually killing the old "ham" acting by obviating the necessity for it.

The second development—a theoretical one—was the notion that a theatrical production should be something more than one or two star performers exhibiting themselves amongst a lot of third-raters, and this began steadily to gain ground after the 1840's—first as the natural answer to a dearth of great actors, and secondly, as a spontaneous reaction to the disadvantages of the star system itself. Cooke and Kean were undoubtedly actors of genius, but you could never be sure when "potations pottle-deep" might render them incoherent or completely incapable, and spoil the whole evening's fun. In addition to this, the intellectual leanings of Macready, the studious common sense of Samuel Phelps, and the strong antiquarian bent of Kean's son, Charles, led them all, for various reasons, to consider a play as a whole and not simply as a vehicle for personal exhibition. Macready and Phelps were the first leading actors deliberately to cast themselves in secondary roles for the good of the play, and Macready was the first actor to fill his company with players who were all his equals in their own line of work. Writing in 1886, Phelps says, "I doubt whether at any time the works of our great masters have ever received in their entirety such perfect illustration in every detail as they obtained during the matchless management of William Charles Macready."

STROLLING AND BARNSTORMING

HITHERTO, we have neglected those most important forms of theatrical activity—stock acting and strolling. The West End actor may tell you that the Mecca of Theatreland is London, and that the peak of a player's ambition is a nine months' run on Shaftesbury Avenue. But the stock actor, and the one-night-stander, and the tragedian doing the "smalls" of Ireland, and the tyro trying his stage legs in weekly "rep," all know better. They know, as Hazlitt knew, that it is the provincial commencement of a player's career that is "the poetical and truly enviable part of it," and that "no thunder of applause from a brilliant and overflowing London audience can ever equal the light-hearted intoxication of unlooked-for success in a barn."

In *The Taming of the Shrew* (1594), there is a stage direction : "Enter two Players, with packs on their backs"—strollers travelling "hard upon the hoof from village to village for cheese and buttermilk." Two hundred years later, when Samuel Phelps went on the stage, the picture had little altered. Hearing of a company in Lincoln wanting a new juvenile, he borrowed a ringlet wig from a fellow actor "who had been playing heroes but was now going into low comedy," picked up "a pair of russet boots, a pair of sandals, a pair of fleshings, a pair of worsted tights, an old sword, and a few other odds and ends" for 30s., and set off, with his bundle of props slung over his shoulder, to tramp the hundred and fifty-odd miles to the scene of his first engagement. When he arrived, he was taken on at a guinea a week, to open the following night in *Macbeth*, playing Third Witch, Duncan, First Murderer, Ross, one of the Apparitions, the Physician, and the "cream-fac'd loon."

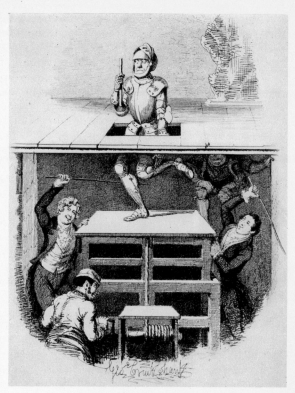

TEASING THE GHOST IN *HAMLET*
Engraving by George Cruikshank, 1857

The stock companies established themselves in the many provincial theatres built between 1725 and 1875 in towns like Bath, Bristol, Exeter, Birmingham, Cheltenham, York, Newcastle and Norwich, and all the players who later won fame and fortune in London received their early grounding in one or other of these companies — Siddons and Dora Jordan at York, Cooke at Liverpool, Kean at Exeter, Macready at Newcastle, and so on. Often the company based itself upon the biggest town in the district, and then worked a circuit of surrounding towns and villages. Thus, the Newcastle company played Scarborough, Durham, Sunderland, North and South Shields, Stockton, Darlington and Coventry, as well as Newcastle itself; while the West Kent circuit comprised Tunbridge Wells, Canterbury, Dover, Maidstone, Faversham and Rochester.

The companies performed the London repertoire with scarcely any variation—indeed variation was out of the question, for they received frequent visits from London stars, who expected stage business and positions to be exactly the same as at Drury Lane or Covent Garden. It is said that when Barry Sullivan arrived in Sheffield with a very bad cold, and was asked by the local stage manager when he would like to rehearse with the resident company, he said that he had no intention of rehearsing in his present condition. When reminded that the week's

39

repertoire was a very stiff one—*Hamlet* on Monday, *Richard III* on Tuesday, *Macbeth* on Wednesday, etc.—and that the company would at least like a word or two of instruction, he replied, "Instruction my foot! Tell them all to keep six feet away from me, and be damned to them!"

The provincial theatres were mostly small, and therefore far easier to play in than the great barns which were put up later. A perfect example is Theatre Royal, Bristol, built towards the end of the eighteenth century, recently rescued from the auctioneer's hammer, and restored more or less to its original condition. A much smaller one is the little Richmond Theatre in Yorkshire—lately re-discovered and partly renovated. Theatre Royal, Bristol, holds about six hundred people, and the Richmond Theatre about two hundred. All the great stars of the late eighteenth and early nineteenth centuries regularly played both these dates.

The strolling player gave a show wherever he could find an audience. One little band in the early eighteenth century performed in a half-clean stable, in which the pig-sty, "not entirely free from the scent of its usual inhabitants," was the only dressing room. Another company used a bed-room for a theatre, with a large four-poster bed for a stage! Speeches from various plays were often so jumbled up that the oldest members of the company were at a loss to know what play was being performed; but country audiences were none the wiser. On more than one occasion a spectator even took an actor at his word. Thus a farmer, hearing the actor Griffiths shouting, "A horse! A horse! My kingdom for a horse!" immediately offered to oblige him with one!

The actor, Bernard, opened his career in a company which had only three male performers. One played tyrants in tragedies and the French horn in the orchestra; the manager prompted, took the money, built and painted the scenery, played the fiddle and made noises off; the third played lovers, sang, danced, and did conjuring tricks. Yet three times a week this heroic brotherhood "put William Shakespeare upon the rack, to the delight of the red-headed bumpkins of Hampshire."

First of all, permission to perform had to be obtained from the local magistrates, and often this permission was refused. In the early 1800's, the reigning magistrate at Romford, Essex, greeted Edward Stirling's humble request to perform a few nights in the Town Hall, with the following speech: "What, sir! Bring your beggarly actors into this town to demoralise the people? No, sir! I will have no such profligacy in Romford. Poor people shall not be wheedled out of their money by your tomfooleries. The first player that comes here, I'll clap him in the stocks as a rogue and vagabond! Good morning, sir!"

Nor had puritanism much abated. In 1792 a Mr. Garrod preached a sermon in Hull, in which he said: "No player, or any of his children, ought to be entitled to a Christian burial, or even to lie in a churchyard. Not one can be saved." Adding as makeweight, "Everyone who enters a

ELLEN TERRY AS LADY MACBETH
Oil painting by John S. Sargent, 1889

LAURENCE OLIVIER AS ROMEO
Oil painting by Harold Knight, 1936

playhouse is, with the players, equally certain of eternal damnation." But in spite of obstacles and opposition, the ancient craft endured, unchanged in many details since the earliest times. Thus the sharing system was preserved amongst the strollers well into the nineteenth century, even candle-ends left over after each performance being equally divided. All parts were hand-written, the single complete script being passed from player to player. Long after railway travel had become quite common, strollers were still padding the hoof, carrying the poles and canvas of their fit-up theatre on their backs.

In the last quarter of the nineteenth century, old-fashioned strolling gave way to "touring," which is strolling minus many of the hazards and many of the joys. But the basic elements of adventure and variety remained, and no actor can remember his touring days without a glow of satisfaction—the Sunday train-calls, the search for "digs," the kippers or pork sausages after the show (with tea or beer, according to taste), the round of second-hand shops and local places of interest, the landlady's tale of past celebrities ("Such a lovely gentleman! He always stayed with me!"), the joys of first love in a double "combined" at 18s. a week (full board for two, 46s.—I speak of the early 1930's!) and, last but not least, the ritual of signing the Visitors' Book—"A Home from Home, shall always recommend!"

The war brought strolling back with a bang, with hazards and joys multiplied a hundredfold; and thousands of actors and actresses discovered for the first time that wherever you are—in camp or canteen, in hangar or hostel, on gun site or searchlight battery, night or day, shine or shower—if a band of willing players meets a hungry audience, there is the theatre in their midst.

So let us salute a single hardy specimen of an ancient and honourable stock—May Hallatt, a 70-year-old actress, who, in the sunset of her professional life, packed her bags and marched across two thousand miles of African sand in the wake of the British Army. She was two years away, her ship was torpedoed on the voyage out, and she lost all her belongings; she went for months at a time without a bath, night after night her bed was the desert, and she arrived home with nothing but the clothes she stood up in and a yak-skin overcoat which had somehow found its way down from the Caucasus into Egypt. She is the type of the eternal, indefatigable, unquenchable trouper, the immemorial "pro," the salt of the theatrical earth.

COMMON SENSE AT LAST?

AFTER the heroic efforts of Macready, Phelps and Irving, nothing remained except thrilling memories. Great figures like Forbes Robertson and Beerbohm Tree toiled hard along the old realistic paths, and if this were simply an essay on actors they and hundreds of others would have a much larger place in it. But the objective to which all these labours pointed was as yet unachieved, and London was still without a theatre or a band of players devoted exclusively to presenting the great classics of the English drama—let alone one devoted to fostering anything bold and adventurous in the way of new plays.

Yet the tide was already beginning to turn, and within the first decade of the present century new and revolutionary forces were beginning to make themselves felt. First of all Shaw and William Archer, assisted by J. T. Grein, succeeded in winning recognition for the new drama, and particularly for Ibsen, its most powerful exponent. This drama introduced quite new concepts into the theatre, by treating serious problems in a serious way, and by assuming that audiences were willing to accept real characters in place of the old stock figures of the Victorian stage. Ibsen was followed by Shaw, and Shaw by Galsworthy, and suddenly the British theatre took on a new lease of life.

The new drama naturally demanded a new approach to the problems of presentation. In the early 1900's the idea began to gain ground that it is better to have someone in charge of a play who stands quite outside it, than for the leading actor to try and look at it from the outside whilst being at the same time locked up inside it. This new function was called "producing," and two men in particular—Gordon Craig and Harley Gran- ville-Barker—working strictly in this new capacity, showed the way towards that unified and balanced mixture of light, music, scenery and actor, which we now recognise as the only possible aim in stage presentation.

Gordon Craig is one of the most important figures in the develop- ment of the twentieth-century theatre. It was his mother, Ellen Terry, who gave him the opportunity to try out his new ideas on stagecraft in the only way possible—by renting a theatre and letting him loose in it. His production of Ibsen's *Vikings*, at the old Imperial Theatre in 1903, started a revolution in the world of *mise en scène* which set the whole European theatre off on a new path ; and we have only to look at one of his models in the Victoria and Albert Musuem to realise his absolute originality in breaking with the deeply-rooted but nonsensical pseudo-realism of the nineteenth century and to understand why his reputation is so great in almost every country but his own.

At the same time, things were stirring in the provinces. In 1907 Miss Horniman launched her famous Repertory Company at the Gaiety Theatre, Manchester. Two years later Alfred Wareing started a similar venture in Glasgow, and 1911 saw the beginnings of repertory in Liverpool. Rejecting the old stock and touring values, these companies set about discovering new plays, finding producers to produce them, and training young and intelligent actors to act them, and one or two of them set standards of acting and production which have never been surpassed in the provincial theatre.

PEGGY ASHCROFT AS ROSALIND IN *AS YOU LIKE IT*
Pencil drawing by W. R. Sickert, 1932

Meanwhile, events of equal importance were happening in the Waterloo Road, S.E.1. In 1880, a Miss Emma Cons, inspired by the efforts of Samuel Phelps in Islington, had conceived the idea of civilising another savage district of London. Taking a lease of the old Coburg Theatre just outside Waterloo Station, she founded what later became known as the Old Vic. For many years programmes were simply a mixture of music, drama and lectures, but in 1914 Lilian Bayliss, who had succeeded to the management on the death of the founder, embarked upon a policy of classical drama at popular prices (5*d.* to 5*s.*). Thereafter, gifted producers like Robert Atkins, Andrew Leigh and Harcourt Williams, aided by such brilliant players as Ion Swinley, Florence Saunders, Baliol Holloway, Sybil Thorndike, Peggy Ashcroft, John Gielgud and Edith Evans, produced a steady flow of Shakespeare, Sheridan, Goldsmith, Dekker, Beaumont and Fletcher, and other classical playwrights, with occasional excursions into the German and Scandinavian drama as makeweight. By 1921, the whole of Shakespeare had been produced and the Old Vic had earned the right to be called the first National Theatre.

Between the two wars Norman Marshall (at the Gate Theatre), Norman MacDermott, Malcolm Morley and Milton Rosmer (at the Everyman),

43

Terence Gray (at the Cambridge Festival), J. B. Fagan (at Oxford), and other imaginative producers, sick to death of the commercial theatre, continued the pioneer work of Shaw and Granville-Barker, only on a much smaller scale and outside the ruinous orbit of the trade theatres. In addition to these, the Sunday Societies—The Phoenix, the Fellowship of Players and the Stage Society—often rehearsed for five or six weeks in order to give two performances of a rarely-acted masterpiece, for which each performer received two guineas to cover bus-fares. Thus the serious drama was kept in being during the most difficult years, and actors and actresses were able to show that they were ready to work their fingers to the bone for a pittance in order to save their souls.

Meanwhile, the repertory companies kept the banner flying in the provinces, and when the theatre seemed to be fighting a losing battle with the cinema, places like Hull, Sheffield, Bristol, Birmingham and York continued to support resident companies in spite of the new craze, although hundreds of touring theatres remained dark, and hundreds of touring actors were walking up and down the Charing Cross Road wondering where their next meal was coming from.

The Second World War, which at first looked like killing the drama stone-dead, actually brought a big theatrical revival, largely stimulated by the Council for Encouragement of Music and the Arts—later called the Arts Council of Great Britain. This was a typical English growth—like the "unofficial rose" of Grantchester—using Pilgrim Trust funds to carry entertainment into those corners of the land which the war and the black-out had suddenly deprived of such comforts. But the Ministry of Information had already used Treasury money to bring Robert Ardrey's play *Thunder Rock* from a tiny theatre in South Kensington into the West End, because it was felt that its message of courage and hope would pay a dividend beyond all reckoning of the box office (actually the Ministry embarrassed itself by making an £ *s. d.* profit as well !) and it was inevitable that sooner or later CEMA would receive Treasury backing. The fact that it did receive it within four months of its foundation meant that for the first time in history the State recognised the drama as one of the sinews of the national soul, and this was the most important thing that had happened to the British theatre since the birth of Shakespeare. There is no question of the theatre not being expected to pay its way. On the contrary, a healthy theatre *should* pay its way. But many a fine play and many a hopeful venture have died in the past because they were asked to obey the iron laws of profit and loss, instead of the laws of public service which put the job first and the possibility of profit second. The new dispensation simply recognises that you cannot treat the theatre as a branch of commerce.

The war drove the Old Vic into the provinces, and sadly battered its ancient home in the Waterloo Road. But its brilliant director, Tyrone Guthrie, kept two or three companies on tour during the darkest and most

EDITH EVANS ABOUT TO MAKE HER ENTRANCE AS QUEEN ELIZABETH
IN HERBERT FARJEON'S *DIVERSION NO. 2*
Drawing by Feliks Topolski, 1940

difficult days, then suddenly returned to London in 1942 with a fine
production of *Othello*, directed by Julius Gellner; and from that time
onwards it continued to cheer and comfort the capital.

45

At the end of the war, Guthrie handed over to Ralph Richardson, a character actor of genius, and Laurence Olivier, a player who combines the vitality and virility of the old with all the sense and subtlety of the new, in a fresh and vigorous blending. These two, ably abetted by John Burrell, have raised the prestige of the Vic once more to its old height, not least among their achievements being the fact that they have drawn to the New Theatre thousands of film fans who have never read a word of Shakespeare, but know it must be good if Larry and Ralph are in it, and who are in any case forming an excellent habit! Thus the cinema is able to repay part of a long-standing debt to its mother art!

We need many new theatres, built and owned by the State, rentable on reasonable terms, and designed on far more flexible lines than the present conventional pattern—with proscenium frame able to be put up or taken down according to the kind of play being produced, thus releasing the drama from its present slavery to the two-dimensional. I think this might actually be the means of bringing back the poetic play into our theatre as a living force. It is a significant fact that nearly every English poet after the 1780's felt a longing to write for the theatre. Wordsworth, Coleridge, Keats, Shelley, Byron, Southey, Scott, Lamb, Landor, Beddoes, and later Browning and Tennyson, all made abortive excursions into the drama, but it was impossible to pick up the threads of the broken tradition, and in any event the theatre had become so debased and commercialised that even Shakespeare was hard put to it to hold his own amongst the waterfalls, elephants, performing dogs, lion-tamers, tightrope-walkers, conjurors and other curiosities which had been allowed to invade the legitimate boards. But to-day the situation is quite different. The theatre is beginning to offer a hope for all sorts of new forms and flourishings, and if our poets will submit to the workshop discipline of the theatre, it may be we shall yet manage to build a poetic drama worthy of the Elizabethan heritage.

We also need to pension off as many of the theatrical adventurers as possible, and return once more to the Elizabethan sharing system which was reverted to during the early years of the war with such success. We need to forget London a little, and think more of the theatre as a whole. Also we need to cut down the price of seats, and make it possible to take a girl friend out for the evening for less than the £5 it costs to-day. Finally, we all need to remember that actors used to be rogues and vagabonds and that an adherence to the more boring forms of society dress and behaviour is only a recent growth and that it has nothing whatever to do with the theatre.

As I look back over these pages I realise how many shades will cut me dead in the Green Rooms of the Elysian Fields where the endless and unresolved debates are continued in an undimmable afterglow of steel-blue and surprise pink—the divine Helen Faucit and Elizabeth O'Neill ; John Quick and Dicky Suett ; Matthews and Liston and Munden and Emery ;

46

JOHN GIELGUD AS VALENTINE IN *LOVE FOR LOVE*
Oil painting by Anthony Devas, 1943

Elliston and handsome Jack Bannister; John Baldwin Buckstone and Little Robson; Woodward and West Digges and Thomas Doggett; Mrs. Mattocks and Mrs. Yates and Perdita Robinson; the Kendals and the Keeleys and the Bancrofts; Hare and Wyndham and Hawtrey and Du Maurier and hundreds of others. But many of them have written about themselves, and

47

other people have written most delightfully about the rest. The second-hand book shops are still overflowing with theatrical treasures at knock-down prices.

About a host of living colleagues I feel less guilty. Them you can still see and hear. Them you can still laugh and cry with. Them you can still love in the flesh.

The present situation is full of hope. We may be poor in dollars, but I believe we have never before been so rich in non-material energies, and I believe that the theatre can play a more important part than ever before in guiding and expressing the present spirit of aspiration and adventure.

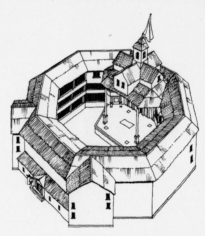

SHAKESPEARE'S GLOBE THEATRE

SHORT BIBLIOGRAPHY

An Apology for the life of Mr. Colley Cibber, Comedian by Colley Cibber. 1740, London.—*Memoirs of his own life* by Tate Wilkinson. 4 vols. 1790, York.—*The Itinerant, or Memoirs of an Actor* by S. W. Ryley. 9 vols. 1808-27, London.—*A View of the English Stage* by William Hazlitt. 1818, London.—"*Their Majesties' Servants*" by John Doran. 2 vols. 1864, London.—*On Actors and the Art of Acting* by G. H. Lewes. 1875, London.—*Macready's Reminiscences, and selections from his diaries and letters* by Sir F. Pollock, Bt. (ed.). 2 vols. 1875, London.—*Our Old Actors* by H. Barton Baker. 2 vols. 1878, London.—*Dramatic Opinions and Essays* by G. B. Shaw. 1907, Constable.—*The Story of My Life* by Ellen Terry. 1908, Hutchinson (reprinted as *Ellen Terry's Memoirs*, 1933, Gollancz).—*Edmund Kean* by H. N. Hillebrand. 1933, Columbia University Press.—*The Globe Playhouse* by John Cranford Adams. 1942, Harvard University Press